Michigan Bingo Book

COMPLETE BINGO GAME IN A BOOK

I0155217

E PLURIBUS UNUM

TUEBOR

SI QUÆRIS PENINSULAM AMŒNAM

CIRCUMSPICE

Written By Rebecca Stark

ISBN 978-0-87386-515-9

Educational Books 'n' Bingo

Printed in the U.S.A.

TERMS INCLUDED

John Jacob Astor

Automotive

Battle Creek

Border(s)

Antoine de la Mothe Cadillac

Civil War

Climate

County (-ies)

Dairy

Detroit

Dwarf Lake Iris

Executive Branch

Fisheries

Flag

Gerald Ford

Henry Ford

French and Indian War

Grand Rapids

Great Lakes

Great Lakes Plain(s)

Isle Royal Greenstone

Judicial Branch

René Robert Cavelier, Sieur de La Salle

Lake St. Clair

Lansing

Legislative Branch

Lower Peninsula

Lumber

Mackinac

Mastodon

Mining (-ed)

Motto (-es)

Mount Arvon

Northwest Territory

Painted Turtle

Peninsulas

Petoskey Stone

Pontiac

Rivers

Robin

Sault Ste. Marie

Seal

Superior Upland

Territory of Michigan

Tribe(s)

Underground Railroad

Union

University of Michigan

Upper Peninsula

White Pine

Additional Terms

Choose as many additional terms as you would like and write them in the squares. Repeat each as desired.

Cut out the squares and randomly distribute them to the class.

Instruct the students to place their square on the center space of their card.

Clues for
Additional Terms

Write three clues for each of your additional terms.

_____ 1. 2. 3.	_____ 1. 2. 3.
_____ 1. 2. 3.	_____ 1. 2. 3.
_____ 1. 2. 3.	_____ 1. 2. 3.

John Jacob Astor
1. This German immigrant came to America after the American Revolution. He built a fur-trading empire.
2. In 1808 ___ founded the American Fur Company. He was the first multi-millionaire in the United States.

Automotive
1. The ___ industry is Michigan's most valuable manufacturing sector.
2. The ___ industry designs, develops, manufactures, markets, and sells motor vehicles.

Battle Creek
1. The Kellogg Company's world headquarters are located in ___.
2. ___ is known as "The Cereal Capital."

Border(s)
1. Wisconsin, Indiana, and Ohio ___ Michigan.
2. Four of the five Great Lakes ___ Michigan.

Antoine de la Mothe Cadillac
1. In 1694 this French explorer was put in charge of the frontier post at Mackinac.
2. ___ founded Detroit in 1701. It was called Fort Pontchartrain du Dètroit. *Dètroit* was the French word for "strait."

Civil War
1. Michigan fought on the side of the Union during the ___.
2. Although far from the fighting during the ___, Michigan helped by supplying the Union with large number of troops.

Climate
1. The southern and central parts of the Lower Peninsula have a warmer ___ than the rest of the state. These areas have hot summers and cold winters.
2. The Upper Peninsula and the northern part of the Lower Peninsula have a more severe climate. These areas have warm, but shorter summers and longer, cold to very cold winters.

County (-ies)
1. There are 83 ___ in Michigan.
2. Wayne is the largest ___ in population. The ___ seat is Detroit.

Dairy
1. About 1/4 of Michigan's agricultural revenues are from ___ products, especially milk and cheese.
2. Michigan ranks second among all states in the production of ___ products.

Detroit
1. It is the largest city in Michigan.
2. From 1805 to 1837 ___ was the capital of the Territory of Michigan. From 1837 to 1847 it was the state capital.

Dwarf Lake Iris 1. The apple blossom is the state flower. The ___ is the state *wildflower*. 2. This wildflower, which is found in parts of the Great Lakes Region, is very rare.	**Executive Branch** 1. The ___ comprises the governor, the lieutenant governor, the secretary of state, and the attorney general. Various departments are also part of this branch. 2. The governor is head of the ___. The present-day ___ is [fill in].
Fisheries 1. Both commercial and sport ___ are important industries in the Great Lakes region. 2. The most important catches for commercial ___ include whitefish, smelt, walleye, and perch. The most popular catches for sport anglers include salmon, steelhead, walleye, lake trout, perch and bass.	**Flag** 1. The state ___ contains the state coat of arms centered on a blue field. 2. The state coat of arms appears on both sides of the ___. Animal symbols on the coat of arms include a moose and an elk to represent Michigan and a bald eagle to represent the United States.
Gerald Ford 1. ___, a former congressman from Grand Rapids, was the 38th President of the United States. 2. ___ was the first vice president chosen under the terms of the 25th Amendment. He was also the first to succeed a President who resigned.	**Henry Ford** 1. ___ established the Ford Motor Company in Detroit in1903. His introduction of the Model T automobile revolutionized transportation and American industry. 2. ___ is best known for his role in the development of the assembly-line technique of mass production.
French and Indian War 1. In the ___, British and American soldiers fought French and Native American soldiers for control of North America. 2. The Treaty of Paris of 1763 ended the ___. The British took control of the lands that had been claimed by France, including what is now Michigan.	**Grand Rapids** 1. By the 1800s, this city was called "America's Furniture Capital." 2. This city on the Grand River is the second largest city in Michigan.
Great Lakes 1. Four of the five ___ border Michigan. They are Lake Superior, Lake Michigan, Lake Huron, and Lake Erie. 2. Michigan is called the "___ State." Ontario is the only one that does not border Michigan.	**Great Lakes Plain(s)** 1. All but the western part of the Upper Peninsula is in the ___ region. 2. The land region known as the ___ stretches along the Great Lakes, from Michigan and Wisconsin to Ohio.

Michigan Bingo

Isle Royal Greenstone

1. Sometimes called the green starstone, the ___ is the state gem. When polished, this stone has a turtleback pattern.
2. The scientific name for this bluish-green gemstone is *chlorastrolite.*

Judicial Branch

1. The ___ interprets what our laws mean. It makes decisions about the laws and those who break them.
2. The ___ is made up of several courts, the highest of which is the state Supreme Court.

René Robert Cavelier, Sieur de La Salle

1. ___ led an expedition down the Mississippi River.
2. ___ claimed the entire Mississippi River basin for France and named it Louisiana after King Louis XIV.

Lake St. Clair

1. This freshwater lake was named after Clare of Assisi.
2. ___ is in the Great Lakes system, but it is not considered one of the Great Lakes. It lies between the Province of Ontario and the State of Michigan.

Lansing

1. ___ is the capital of Michigan.
2. It is one of the few state capitals that is not also a county seat.

Legislative Branch

1. The ___ of government comprises the Senate and the House of Representatives.
2. The ___ makes the laws.

Lower Peninsula

1. The ___ is surrounded by water on all sides except its southern border, which it shares with Ohio and Indiana. Its water boundaries are Lake Michigan, Lake Huron, Lake St. Clair, and Lake Erie.
2. The shape of the ___ resembles that of a mitten.

Lumber

1. Between 1869 and 1900, Michigan was the nation's leading producer of ___. White pine, which was in high demand for construction, grew in abundance in northern Michigan.
2. Two innovations of the 1870s contributed to the large increases in ___ production: logging wheels and the narrow-gauge railroad.

Mackinac

1. The Straits of ___ is the strip of water that connects Lake Michigan and Lake Huron and separates the Lower and Upper peninsulas. A suspension bridge spans the straits.
2. ___ Island was the second national park in the United States, preceded only by Yellowstone.

Mastodon

1. The giant ___ is the official state fossil.
2. One of the most complete ___ skeletons ever found was discovered near Owosso, Michigan.

Michigan Bingo

Mining (-ed) 1. Michigan's most important ___ products are natural gas, iron ore and petroleum. 2. The ___ industry is important. Michigan ranks second in the production of iron ore and has one of the world's largest limestone quarries.	**Motto (-es** 1. *"Si Quaeris Peninsulam Amoenam, Circumspice"* is the state ___. 2. The state ___ is in Latin. In English it means, "If you seek a pleasant peninsula, look about you."
Mount Arvon 1. At 1,979 feet, ___ is the highest point in the state. 2. Complete this analogy: Lowest Point : Lake Erie :: Highest Point : ___	**Northwest Territory** 1. The ___ comprised the modern states of Ohio, Indiana, Illinois, Michigan, Wisconsin, and the northeastern part of Minnesota. 2. As part of the Jay Treaty of 1794, Britain agreed to leave the ___.
Painted Turtle 1. The ___ is the state reptile. 2. This reptile lives in slow-moving, fresh waters.	**Peninsulas** 1. Michigan is divided into the Upper and Lower ___. 2. The Upper and Lower ___ are separated by the Straits of Mackinac.
Petoskey Stone 1. The ___ has been designated the state stone. 2. The ___ is actually fossilized coral.	**Pontiac** 1. This Ottawa Indian chief was a great intertribal leader; he organized a combined resistance which became known as ___'s War. 2. In 1762 ___ enlisted support from other tribes in the Great Lakes area to expel the British.
River(s) 1. The Detroit, Grand, Kalamazoo, St. Clair, and St. Marys are ___ in Michigan. 2. The Grand ___ is the longest one Michigan. It runs through the cities of Jackson, Eaton Rapids, Lansing, Grand Rapids, and Grand Haven. Michigan Bingo	**Robin** 1. The ___ is the state bird. It was chosen by the Michigan Audubon Society. 2. The legislation designating the ___ as the state bird included this statement: "The ___ is the best known and best loved of all the birds in the State of Michigan." © Barbara M. Peller

Sault Ste. Marie
1. In 1668 Father Jacques Marquette founded the first permanent settlement on Michigan soil at ___.
2. The Soo Locks are on the St. Marys River in ___. These parallel locks make it possible for ships to travel between Lake Superior and the lower Great Lakes.

Seal
1. Three mottoes appear on both the state coat of arms and the Great ___ of Michigan.
2. A moose, an elk, and a bald eagle are on both the coat of arms and the Great ___.

Superior Upland
1. The western area of the Upper Peninsula is in the region referred to as ___.
2. The land in the ___ region has higher elevations and a more rugged terrain than in the Great Lakes Plain.

Territory of Michigan
1. The ___ was created in 1805. Before that, Michigan was part of the Territory of Indiana.
2. The ___ was in existence from June 30, 1805, until January 26, 1837. Detroit was its capital.

Tribe(s)
1. The Fox, Huron, Kickapoo, Menominee, Miami, Ojibwe, Ottawa, Potawatomi and Sauk are ___ of Michigan.
2. The Saginaw Chippewa Indian ___ lives in central Michigan. Their tribal government offices are on the Isabella Indian Reservation, near the city of Mount Pleasant.

Underground Railroad
1. The ___ was a network of secret routes and safe houses used by slaves to escape to free states.
2. Many Michigan citizens helped slaves escape from the South via the ___.

Union
1. When Michigan was admitted to the ___ on January 26, 1837, it became the 26th state.
2. In 1837 Michigan was admitted to the ___ as a free state, and Arkansas was admitted as a slave state.

University of Michigan
1. The flagship campus of the ___ is located in Ann Arbor.
2. The athletic teams of the ___ are called the Wolverines.

Upper Peninsula
1. The ___ is bounded on the north by Lake Superior, on the east by the St. Marys River, on the southeast by Lake Michigan and Lake Huron, and on the southwest by Wisconsin.
2. The ___ is sometimes referred to as "above the bridge."

White Pine
1. The eastern ___ is the official state tree.
2. This evergreen tree has bluish-green to medium-green needles.

Michigan Bingo

Michigan Bingo

River(s)	John Jacob Astor	Battle Creek	Grand Rapids	Antoine de la Mothe Cadillac
Motto (-es)	Automotive	Mining (-ed)	Mackinac	Seal
University of Michigan	Lumber		Peninsulas	Upper Peninsula
Union	Sault Ste. Marie	Underground Railroad	Lower Peninsula	Mount Arvon
Painted Turtle	Isle Royal Greenstone	Flag	Territory of Michigan	Lake St. Clair

Michigan Bingo: Card No. 1

Michigan Bingo

Union	University of Michigan	René Robert Cavelier, Sieur de La Salle	Robin	Legislative Branch
Mount Arvon	Gerald Ford	County (-ies)	Sault Ste. Marie	Northwest Territory
Detroit	Isle Royal Greenstone		Judicial Branch	Underground Railroad
Petoskey Stone	Pontiac	Lumber	White Pine	Antoine de la Mothe Cadillac
Seal	Mining (-ed)	Flag	Motto (-es)	Territory of Michigan

Michigan Bingo

Isle Royal Greenstone	Underground Railroad	Gerald Ford	Lower Peninsula	University of Michigan
Mount Arvon	Automotive	Dairy	John Jacob Astor	Great Lakes Plain(s)
Sault Ste. Marie	Mining (-ed)		Northwest Territory	Border(s)
Lumber	Detroit	Painted Turtle	Petoskey Stone	René Robert Cavelier, Sieur de La Salle
Territory of Michigan	Dwarf Lake Iris	Flag	White Pine	Legislative Branch

Michigan Bingo

Lumber	Northwest Territory	Battle Creek	Dwarf Lake Iris	Legislative Branch
Mastodon	Climate	John Jacob Astor	Robin	University of Michigan
Peninsulas	Petoskey Stone		Lake St. Clair	Grand Rapids
Underground Railroad	Automotive	Mining (-ed)	Flag	County (-ies)
Executive Branch	Seal	Civil War	Territory of Michigan	Upper Peninsula

Michigan Bingo

Seal	Antoine de la Mothe Cadillac	Sault Ste. Marie	County (-ies)	Dwarf Lake Iris
Mastodon	Underground Railroad	Dairy	Judicial Branch	Automotive
Battle Creek	Upper Peninsula		Mackinac	Great Lakes
Lake St. Clair	Legislative Branch	River(s)	White Pine	Fisheries
Gerald Ford	Flag	University of Michigan	Lumber	Peninsulas

Michigan Bingo: Card No. 5

Michigan Bingo

Border(s)	Northwest Territory	René Robert Cavelier, Sieur de La Salle	Legislative Branch	Upper Peninsula
Lower Peninsula	Sault Ste. Marie	Fisheries	John Jacob Astor	University of Michigan
Robin	Executive Branch		Climate	Judicial Branch
Flag	Painted Turtle	White Pine	Civil War	Battle Creek
Mount Arvon	County (-ies)	River(s)	Peninsulas	Henry Ford

Michigan Bingo

River(s)	Northwest Territory	Great Lakes	Underground Railroad	Gerald Ford
Mount Arvon	Legislative Branch	Isle Royal Greenstone	Automotive	Mastodon
Upper Peninsula	Grand Rapids		Judicial Branch	Climate
Lumber	Petoskey Stone	Dairy	Union	Detroit
Flag	Dwarf Lake Iris	White Pine	Civil War	Border(s)

Michigan Bingo: Card No. 7

Michigan Bingo

Peninsulas	Northwest Territory	French and Indian War	Lower Peninsula	Climate
Mastodon	Battle Creek	Robin	Upper Peninsula	County (-ies)
Henry Ford	Dwarf Lake Iris		Legislative Branch	Antoine de la Mothe Cadillac
Territory of Michigan	Lumber	Union	Executive Branch	Petoskey Stone
Mining (-ed)	Flag	Civil War	Sault Ste. Marie	Mount Arvon

Michigan Bingo

Judicial Branch	Gerald Ford	Isle Royal Greenstone	Henry Ford	Dwarf Lake Iris
Executive Branch	Legislative Branch	Peninsulas	Sault Ste. Marie	Northwest Territory
Great Lakes Plain(s)	River(s)		Automotive	French and Indian War
Fisheries	Antoine de la Mothe Cadillac	Painted Turtle	Mackinac	Great Lakes
Petoskey Stone	White Pine	Dairy	Union	Lake St. Clair

Michigan Bingo

Union	Lower Peninsula	Climate	Robin	Henry Ford
Upper Peninsula	County (-ies)	John Jacob Astor	Automotive	Legislative Branch
Dwarf Lake Iris	Northwest Territory		Grand Rapids	Detroit
Painted Turtle	Lake St. Clair	Fisheries	White Pine	Great Lakes Plain(s)
Dairy	Mount Arvon	René Robert Cavelier, Sieur de La Salle	Seal	Peninsulas

Michigan Bingo

Border(s)	Northwest Territory	Sault Ste. Marie	Fisheries	Mount Arvon
French and Indian War	Great Lakes Plain(s)	Mackinac	Judicial Branch	John Jacob Astor
Mastodon	Legislative Branch		René Robert Cavelier, Sieur de La Salle	Isle Royal Greenstone
Dairy	University of Michigan	White Pine	Dwarf Lake Iris	Union
Executive Branch	Flag	River(s)	Civil War	Gerald Ford

Michigan Bingo: Card No. 11

Michigan Bingo

Gerald Ford	Antoine de la Mothe Cadillac	Great Lakes Plain(s)	Lower Peninsula	Judicial Branch
Isle Royal Greenstone	Mount Arvon	Battle Creek	Civil War	Automotive
River(s)	Great Lakes		Upper Peninsula	Robin
Flag	Petoskey Stone	Legislative Branch	Union	Mastodon
Northwest Territory	French and Indian War	Dwarf Lake Iris	Executive Branch	County (-ies)

Michigan Bingo

Fisheries	Antoine de la Mothe Cadillac	Border(s)	Great Lakes Plain(s)	Upper Peninsula
Battle Creek	French and Indian War	Legislative Branch	Judicial Branch	Detroit
Lower Peninsula	County (-ies)		Isle Royal Greenstone	Great Lakes
Peninsulas	White Pine	Climate	Dwarf Lake Iris	Union
Flag	Lake St. Clair	Civil War	River(s)	Mackinac

Michigan Bingo

Motto (-es)	Legislative Branch	Sault Ste. Marie	Judicial Branch	Executive Branch
County (-ies)	River(s)	Great Lakes Plain(s)	Automotive	Northwest Territory
Fisheries	Grand Rapids		René Robert Cavelier, Sieur de La Salle	Dairy
Lake St. Clair	White Pine	Dwarf Lake Iris	Climate	Border(s)
Flag	Robin	Detroit	Mount Arvon	Peninsulas

Michigan Bingo

Mackinac	Judicial Branch	Sault Ste. Marie	Gerald Ford	Lower Peninsula
Border(s)	René Robert Cavelier, Sieur de La Salle	John Jacob Astor	Battle Creek	Executive Branch
Upper Peninsula	River(s)		University of Michigan	Northwest Territory
Flag	Great Lakes Plain(s)	French and Indian War	White Pine	Fisheries
Mount Arvon	Petoskey Stone	Civil War	Henry Ford	Isle Royal Greenstone

Michigan Bingo

Climate	Great Lakes Plain(s)	French and Indian War	Henry Ford	Pontiac
Robin	Detroit	Great Lakes	Mastodon	Grand Rapids
Fisheries	Antoine de la Mothe Cadillac		Upper Peninsula	Isle Royal Greenstone
Lumber	County (-ies)	Flag	Mackinac	Union
Executive Branch	Tribe(s)	Civil War	Petoskey Stone	Northwest Territory

Michigan
Bingo

Dairy	Superior Upland	Lansing	Great Lakes Plain(s)	Motto (-es)
Mackinac	Executive Branch	White Pine	Grand Rapids	Great Lakes
Judicial Branch	Peninsulas		Tribe(s)	French and Indian War
Lake St. Clair	Mount Arvon	Union	Sault Ste. Marie	Detroit
Painted Turtle	Fisheries	Gerald Ford	Lower Peninsula	Antoine de la Mothe Cadillac

Michigan Bingo: Card No. 17

Michigan Bingo

Henry Ford	Dwarf Lake Iris	County (-ies)	Fisheries	Robin
Northwest Territory	Dairy	Painted Turtle	Upper Peninsula	Executive Branch
Judicial Branch	Detroit		Lansing	Battle Creek
Antoine de la Mothe Cadillac	John Jacob Astor	White Pine	Union	René Robert Cavelier, Sieur de La Salle
Tribe(s)	Great Lakes Plain(s)	Sault Ste. Marie	Superior Upland	Border(s)

Michigan Bingo

Upper Peninsula	Border(s)	Great Lakes Plain(s)	French and Indian War	Union
Mackinac	Lower Peninsula	Northwest Territory	Gerald Ford	Grand Rapids
Superior Upland	Dwarf Lake Iris		Automotive	University of Michigan
René Robert Cavelier, Sieur de La Salle	Tribe(s)	Painted Turtle	Petoskey Stone	Lansing
Battle Creek	Pontiac	Mount Arvon	Peninsulas	Civil War

Michigan Bingo

Motto (-es)	Superior Upland	Lower Peninsula	Great Lakes Plain(s)	Civil War
County (-ies)	Isle Royal Greenstone	Mastodon	Painted Turtle	Robin
Antoine de la Mothe Cadillac	Great Lakes		Lumber	John Jacob Astor
Seal	Mining (-ed)	Territory of Michigan	Petoskey Stone	Tribe(s)
Underground Railroad	Peninsulas	Pontiac	Union	Lansing

Michigan Bingo

Mackinac	Border(s)	Mastodon	Great Lakes Plain(s)	Seal
Antoine de la Mothe Cadillac	Lansing	Climate	French and Indian War	River(s)
Detroit	Mount Arvon		Superior Upland	Sault Ste. Marie
Painted Turtle	Gerald Ford	Tribe(s)	Lake St. Clair	Peninsulas
Lumber	Pontiac	Civil War	Dairy	Petoskey Stone

Michigan Bingo

Henry Ford	René Robert Cavelier, Sieur de La Salle	Lansing	Battle Creek	Fisheries
Robin	Lower Peninsula	University of Michigan	French and Indian War	Automotive
County (-ies)	Grand Rapids		River(s)	Great Lakes
Tribe(s)	Lake St. Clair	Petoskey Stone	John Jacob Astor	Mastodon
Pontiac	Dairy	Superior Upland	Detroit	Mount Arvon

Michigan Bingo

Climate	Superior Upland	Gerald Ford	Battle Creek	Civil War
Border(s)	Motto (-es)	Mount Arvon	Mackinac	John Jacob Astor
René Robert Cavelier, Sieur de La Salle	Fisheries		Territory of Michigan	River(s)
Detroit	Pontiac	Tribe(s)	Dairy	Petoskey Stone
Seal	Mining (-ed)	Peninsulas	Painted Turtle	Lansing

Michigan Bingo

Climate	Peninsulas	Motto (-es)	Superior Upland	French and Indian War
Lansing	Civil War	Mastodon	Robin	River(s)
Great Lakes	Henry Ford		Fisheries	Detroit
Seal	Territory of Michigan	Tribe(s)	Dairy	Antoine de la Mothe Cadillac
Underground Railroad	Lumber	Pontiac	Lower Peninsula	Mining (-ed)

Michigan Bingo: Card No. 24

Michigan Bingo

Lumber	Mastodon	Superior Upland	Sault Ste. Marie	Lansing
John Jacob Astor	Antoine de la Mothe Cadillac	Mackinac	Climate	Automotive
Lake St. Clair	French and Indian War		Territory of Michigan	Tribe(s)
University of Michigan	Seal	Mining (-ed)	Pontiac	Grand Rapids
Civil War	Motto (-es)	County (-ies)	Executive Branch	Underground Railroad

Michigan Bingo

Lansing	Superior Upland	René Robert Cavelier, Sieur de La Salle	Robin	Henry Ford
Painted Turtle	Lower Peninsula	French and Indian War	Motto (-es)	Climate
Lake St. Clair	Territory of Michigan		Grand Rapids	Lumber
Dairy	Battle Creek	Seal	Pontiac	Tribe(s)
Great Lakes	Executive Branch	Sault Ste. Marie	Mining (-ed)	Underground Railroad

Michigan Bingo: Card No. 26

Michigan Bingo

René Robert Cavelier, Sieur de La Salle	County (-ies)	Superior Upland	Motto (-es)	Isle Royal Greenstone
Seal	Territory of Michigan	Mackinac	Tribe(s)	Automotive
White Pine	Mining (-ed)		Pontiac	Lumber
Henry Ford	Border(s)	Mastodon	Underground Railroad	John Jacob Astor
Executive Branch	Grand Rapids	Lansing	University of Michigan	Great Lakes

Michigan Bingo: Card No. 27

Michigan Bingo

René Robert Cavelier, Sieur de La Salle	Motto (-es)	University of Michigan	Superior Upland	Climate
Isle Royal Greenstone	Lansing	Territory of Michigan	Robin	Grand Rapids
Mining (-ed)	Detroit		Great Lakes	Painted Turtle
Union	Henry Ford	Mount Arvon	Pontiac	Tribe(s)
Battle Creek	Judicial Branch	Executive Branch	Underground Railroad	Seal

Michigan Bingo

Lansing	Motto (-es)	Henry Ford	Mackinac	Judicial Branch
Petoskey Stone	Painted Turtle	Mastodon	Great Lakes	University of Michigan
Lake St. Clair	Territory of Michigan		Automotive	Superior Upland
Isle Royal Greenstone	Seal	Legislative Branch	Pontiac	Tribe(s)
Climate	French and Indian War	Underground Railroad	Border(s)	Mining (-ed)

Michigan Bingo: Card No. 29

Michigan Bingo

Dwarf Lake Iris	Superior Upland	Robin	Judicial Branch	Tribe(s)
John Jacob Astor	Motto (-es)	René Robert Cavelier, Sieur de La Salle	Grand Rapids	Automotive
Lake St. Clair	Fisheries		Great Lakes	Mastodon
Underground Railroad	Border(s)	Battle Creek	Pontiac	Territory of Michigan
Seal	Upper Peninsula	Mining (-ed)	Lansing	University of Michigan

www.ingramcontent.com/pod-product-compliance
Lightning Source LLC
LaVergne TN
LVHW061338060426
835511LV00014B/1987